THE DAD'S BOOK OF JOKES

Dad Jokes, Bad Jokes, Groaners &
One-Liners

HARRY W. HOOVER JR.

CONTENTS

My grandchildren call me "The Dad" and my wife, "The Mom". So, that's why this is The Dad's Book of Jokes.

Here's how that started:

When my daughter got married, her husband had a five-year-old. The youngster already had a full contingent of grandparents. He knew that we were his stepmother's parents but didn't know what he was supposed to call us.

One day he was at the house trying to find my wife. He came into the living room, looked at me, and asked, "where's...the...the...The Mom!" So, that's when he started calling us The Mom and The Dad. Now, we have two more grandsons who call us this. And, many of our friends and their children call us this as well.

I've been telling them Dad Jokes for years. My youngest grandson once said to me, "if this writing thing doesn't work out, you should become a comedian." The next best thing, I guess, is writing a book, using my dad jokes. So, here it is. I hope you enjoy it.

Harry "The Dad" Hoover

ANIMAL JOKES

Did you hear about the chameleon who couldn't change colors? He had a reptile dysfunction.

What do you call a puzzled African antelope? A Bewilderedbeest.

What did the bunny do when he came in out of the rain? He used a hare dryer.

What's a marsupial's favorite cocktail? A piña koala.

How can you tell which rabbit is oldest? Look for gray hares.

Why were the baby cows mad at their mother? Because she told them it was pasture bedtime.

What's the difference between a coyote and a flea? One howls on the prairie, and other prowls on the hairy.

What do frogs drink? Croak-a-Cola.

Did you hear about the pig performing at the comedy club? He was a total boar.

What did the cow's therapist prescribe for her depression? Moo-d altering drugs.

Did you hear about the man who traded his deer for fireworks? He got the best bang for his buck.

What do you call it when it rains turkeys? Fowl weather.

Why was the rabbit so upset? He was having a bad hare

day.

My son asked why the neighbor's dog was motionless in the front yard. I said, "he's on paws."

What happened to the chicken with hiccups? She laid only scrambled eggs.

When the farm animals robbed the bank, who drove the getaway car? The escape goat.

If a pig loses its voice, is it disgruntled?

What do pigs learn in the army? Ham-to-ham combat.

What do you call a rabbit covered in fleas? Bugs Bunny. ⚔

Did you hear about the farmer's chicken-proof fence? It's impeccable.

Did you hear about the demon-possessed palomino? He needed an ex-horse-cist.

How does a tiny bird with a broken wing manage to land safely? With a sparrowchute.

What do you call an alligator with GPS? A navigator. ⚔

What do frogs wear on their feet? Open toad sandals.

What lies on the ground 100 feet in the air? A dead centipede.

Why did the farmer separate the turkey and the chicken? ⚔

He suspected fowl play.

What do you get when you cross a turkey with a banjo? A turkey that plucks itself.

What did the rooster do to impress the hen? Wrote her poultry.

What's big, beautiful, gray and wears glass slippers? Cinderelephant.

What do you call it when you offer calamari in exchange for a favor? Squid pro quo.

Did you know that ducks make great detectives? They always quack the case.

What do you call someone who believes that a chicken's offspring created the universe? An eggnostic.

What's the difference between a baby duck and a cranky two-year-old? One's a tiny waddler, the other is a whiny toddler.

Where do shrimp go to pick up a little extra cash? The prawn shop.

What do you call a cow with a twitch? Beef jerky.

What does a caterpillar do on New Years Day? Turns over a new leaf!

What do you get when you cross a dog with an antenna?

A Golden Receiver.

What kind of dog gets sad if you feed it cantaloupe? A Melon Collie.

What do you call a cow with two legs? Lean beef.

What do you call a cow with no legs? Ground beef.

Why don't sharks eat clowns? Because they taste funny.

What did one flea say to the other flea when they came out of the movies? "Should we walk home or take a dog?"

What kind of bug tells time? A clock-roach.

What did T-Rex do for a living? Small arms dealer.

What's the most religious bug? The praying mantis.

What did the dog who stole his owner's phone get arrested for? Watching kitty porn.

They had yaks in the zoo's wildebeest exhibit. I'm not falling for fake gnus.

What did the elephant say to the naked man? Cute, but can you pick up peanuts with it?

Did you hear about the man getting rich taking pictures of salmon in human clothing? It's like shooting fish in apparel.

What's the most musical part of the chicken? The drumstick.

Why are elephants never rich? Because they work for peanuts.

What do you get when you cross Bambi with a ghost? Bamboo!

Did you hear about the cow private detective? He specializes in steak outs.

What did the pig say at the beach on a hot summer's day? I'm bacon!

Why did the ants dance on the jelly jar? The lid said, "Twist to open."

What do you call a cow that can't give milk? A milk dud, or an udder failure.

Why did the dog win the storytelling contest? He knew how to paws for effect.

What's the quietest type of dog? The hush puppy.

Where does a hamster go on spring break? Hamsterdam.

What's a frog's favorite game? Croak-et.

Did you hear about the big fight between two silkworms? It ended in a tie.

What do you get when you cross a chicken with a

cement mixer? A brick layer.

Why did the chicken go to the séance? To get to the other side.

What do you call a bear with extreme mood swings? A bi-polar bear.

Did you hear about the man who shot his first turkey? Scared the heck out of everyone in the frozen food section.

What do you get when you cross a pig and a dinosaur? Jurassic Pork.

Why did Noah not fish while he was on the Ark? He only had two worms.

What do you call a hamster with a top hat? Abrahamster Lincoln.

Did you hear about the lion who ate his friends? He had to swallow his pride.

What would happen if pigs could fly? The price of bacon would go up.

What do you call lending money to a bison? A buff-a-loan.

What branch of the military do rabbits join? The Hare Force.

Did you hear about the dog audio expert? He specializes in woofers.

What do you call cows with a sense of humor? Laughing stock.

What do you call a cow diva? Dairy queen.

What kind of magic does a Haitian cow practice? Moo-doo.

What do you call a dissatisfied insect? A grumble bee.

Why did the snake cross the road? To get to the other sssssssside.

Did you hear about the man who played Dad instead of dead when he ran into a grizzly? The bear can now ride a bike without training wheels.

What's the difference between a cat and a frog? A cat has nine lives and a frog croaks every night.

Did you hear about the monkeys who shared an Amazon account? They were Prime Mates.

What did the horse say after it fell? Help, I've fallen and can't giddy-up.

How did Noah see the animals in the Ark at night? He used floodlights.

What happened when 500 hares got loose downtown? Police had to comb the area.

What do you call shaving a crazy sheep? Shear madness.

What do you call an exploding monkey? A baboom!

What do you call an alligator wearing a vest? An investigator.

Where do rabbits eat breakfast? IHOP.

Where do cows go on vacation? Moo Zealand.

Why did the elephants get kicked out of the pool? They kept dropping their trunks.

What do you get when you cross a hammock and a dog? A rocker spaniel.

Why did the bee go to the doctor? He had hives.

What's a frog's favorite flower? A croakus.

Why did the lamb run over the cliff? He didn't see the ewe turn.

What are caterpillars afraid of? Doggerpillars.

1.

APHORISMS AND FUNNY SAYINGS

A fool and his money can throw a helluva party.

A child of five could understand this. Someone fetch a child of five. – Groucho Marx

Never hit a man with glasses. Hit him with something bigger and heavier.

Never miss a good chance to shut up. – Will Rogers

Zombies eat brains. You're safe.

I'm in shape. Round is a shape. – George Carlin

Practice safe eating. Always use condiments.

Be careful about reading books. You may die of a misprint. – Mark Twain

Five days a week my body is a temple. The other two it's an amusement park.

The two most common elements in the universe are hydrogen and stupidity. – Harlan Ellison

Sex is hereditary. If your parents never had it, chances are you won't either.

The best things in life are free. So, how many kittens do you want?

I never forget a face. But in your case, I'll make an exception. – Groucho Marx

Natives who beat drums to drive off evil spirits are the object of scorn to smart Americans who blow horns to break up traffic jams.

I put a dollar in a change machine. Nothing changed.

If I were two-faced, would I be wearing this one? – Abraham Lincoln

My imaginary friend says that you need a therapist.

The human brain is a wonderful thing. It starts working the moment you are born and never stops until you stand up to speak in public.

The difference between stupidity and genius is that genius has its limits. – Albert Einstein

It's not whether you win or lose, but how you place the blame.

If had a dollar for every smart thing you say. I'd be poor.

In wine there is wisdom, in beer, there is Freedom, in water, there is bacteria.- Benjamin Franklin

If I wanted to kill myself I would climb your ego and jump to your IQ.

Some cause happiness wherever they go. Others, whenever they go.

A computer once beat me at chess, but it was no match

for me at kickboxing. – Emo Philllips

We have enough youth. How about a fountain of smart.

You can't make people change. Unless you work at a cash register.

Money isn't everything, but it sure keeps the kids in touch.

Clothes make the man. Naked people have little or no influence in society. – Mark Twain

If ignorance is bliss. You must be the happiest person on this planet.

Common sense is like deodorant. The people who need it most never use it.

Anyone who lives within their means suffers from a lack of imagination. – Oscar Wilde

Everyone seems normal until you get to know them.

Reality is only an illusion that occurs due to a lack of alcohol.

We are born naked, wet, and hungry. Then things get worse.

Be yourself. Everyone else is taken – Oscar Wilde

It's OK if you don't like me. Not everyone can have excellent taste.

It's lucky that mirrors can't talk, and in your case, lucky they can't laugh.

A politician is like a banana: first, he's green, then yellow, and finally rotten.

Opportunity is missed by most people because it is dressed in overalls and looks like work. – Thomas Edison

You look good when your eyes are closed, but you look the best when my eyes closed.

I don't believe in plastic surgery. But in your case, go ahead.

2.

CHILDREN JOKES

At the mall, I saw a kid on a leash. Apparently, you are not supposed to ask if it is a rescue.

What's the best way to keep your kids out of hot water? Put some dishes in it.

My mother said, "You won't amount to anything because you procrastinate." I said, "Just you wait."

In school I was never the class clown, but more the class trapeze artist…I was always being suspended.

A baby first laughs at the age of four weeks. By that time his eyes focus well enough to see you clearly.

Summer vacation is a time when parents realize that teachers are grossly underpaid.

How can you tell when you are in a midlife crisis? When your clothes and your children are the same age.

Did you hear about the boy who kept getting electrocuted? His dad grounded him.

What do you call a child whose parents are from Iceland and Cuba? An Ice Cube.

Did you hear about the kid who cut himself on the cheese? It was extra-sharp cheddar.

Why can't orphans go on school field trips? No parent signatures.

Why aren't orphans good at baseball? They can't find home.

"What's this," the woman asked her grandson when he handed her a cup of coffee with an Army man in it. He replied, "the best part of waking up is soldiers in your cup."

Did you hear about the kid who fell into wet cement? He left a bad impression.

Did you hear about the kid who took the school bus home? The police made him bring it back.

What did little Johnny say when his teacher asked what was his favorite bird? He replied, "fried chicken."

The exasperated teacher asked little Johnny why he was doing so poorly in geography. Johnny said his Dad told him the world was changing every day, so he decided to let it settle down before trying to figure out where everything is.

What did little Sally say when the teacher asked her about the Dead Sea? Sally replied, "gosh, I didn't even know it was sick."

What did the first-grader say when his Mom asked him what he learned today? "Not enough," he said. I have to go back tomorrow."

What did Little Johnny say when the fireman asked if he

knew what a smoke alarm was for? Johnny said, "Yes. That's how my Mom knows when dinner is ready."

3

CHRISTMAS JOKES

Why didn't Santa Claus come down any chimneys this year? He forgot to get his flue shot.

What do you call Santa's little helper? Subordinate clauses.

Why did Santa send one of his little helpers to the psychiatrist? Because he had low elf-esteem.

How does Santa keep track of all the fireplaces he has visited? He keeps a log.

What did Santa say when he put the bow on the last package? That's a wrap.

Why is Christmas just like another day at the office? You do all the work and the fat guy in the suit gets all the credit.

What do you call a bad kid who doesn't believe in Santa?

A rebel without a Claus.

What do African animals sing at Christmas time? Jungle Bells.

What do snowmen usually wear on their heads? Ice caps!

What's the difference between Santa's reindeer and a knight? One slays the dragon, and the other's draggin' the sleigh.

What did the husband say when his wife brought in the wrong type Christmas tree? Birch, please!

What's green, covered in tinsel and goes "ribbet, ribbet"? A mistle-toad.

What happens to elves when they are naughty? Santa gives them the sack.

Did you know that Rudolph the Reindeer never went to school? He was elf taught.

What does Santa suffer from if he gets stuck in a chimney? Claustrophobia!

What do you get if you combine Santa and a duck? A Christmas Quacker!

What falls at the North Pole but never gets hurt? Snow.

What do you call Frosty the Snowman in May? A puddle!

What do Santa's little helpers learn at school? The elf-abet.

What type of cars do elves drive? Toy-otas.

What do you call a broke Santa? Saint-NICKEL-LESS.

What do you get if you eat Christmas decorations? Tinselitis.

What do you call a Santa who lives in Los Angeles? A lost Claus.

What's red, white, and blue? A sad candy cane.

What do you get when you cross a snowman and a vampire? Frostbite.

How do Mexican sheep say Merry Christmas? Fleece Navidad.

What do you get if you deep fry Santa? Crisp Kringle.

What's a squirrel's favorite Christmas show? The Nutcracker.

When Santa ran out of coal, what did he give the bad kids? Cleveland Browns' season tickets.

What happened when the man took the advice of the song, Deck The Halls? The Halls are in the ER, the man is in jail.

What's the worst thing about office Christmas parties?

Having to look for a new job the next day.

What do you call it when a snowman throws a temper tantrum? A meltdown.

What do Santa's little helpers eat for lunch on a very cold day? Elf-abet soup.

What's the best thing to put into a Christmas cake? Your teeth.

If an athlete gets athlete's foot, what does an elf get? Mistletoe.

What happens when Santa forgets to put on his underwear? You get Saint Knickerless.

Who steals things from the rich, gift wraps them, and gives them to the poor? Ribbon Hood.

4.

FOOD JOKES

The Dad's Book of Jokes

Did you hear how they caught the famous produce bandit? He stopped to take a leek.

Where did the lettuce go to get a drink after work? The Salad Bar.

What does a British nuclear scientist have for lunch? Fission chips.

What do you call Buddhist tubers? Medi-taters.

Why did the coffee taste like dirt? Because it was ground just a few minutes ago.

Did you see the movie about a hot dog? It was an Oscar Wiener.

How is bread likes the sun? It rises in the yeast and sets in the waist.

What did the celery say to the vegetable dip? I'm stalking you.

Did you hear about the guy who got gas for $1.39? He ate at Taco Bell.

What's green and slimy and has its own talk show? Okra Winfrey.

How do you make pig jerky? Give them some coffee.

What's a pickle's favorite TV game show? Let's Make A Dill.

ver wondered: Why do zombies eat brains?
or thought.

What did the gingerbread man put on his bed? A cookie sheet.

I asked the tiny butcher to get me a couple of ribeyes from the top shelf. He said the steaks are too high.

What vegetable isn't allowed on cruise ships? Leeks.

What do you call a philosophical monk who cooks at McDonald's? A deep friar.

What's a baker's favorite type of joke? Cinnamon puns.

Where do pickles go on vacation? Philadillphia.

Why wouldn't the baker ever sit down? He had sticky buns.

What does an Irishman get after eating Italian food? Gaelic breath.

What does a thesaurus eat for breakfast? A synonym roll.

What do you call the panic-buying of sausage and cheese in Germany? The Wurst Käse scenario.

Did you hear about the explosion at the French cheese factory? De brie was everywhere.

Did you hear about the new restaurant called Karma?

There's no menu...you get what you deserve.

What's the difference between roast beef and pea soup? Anyone can roast beef.

What is a tree's favorite soda? Root beer.

What dessert is best for eating in bed? A sheet cake.

Why couldn't the sesame seed leave the casino? He was on a roll.

What do you call it when strawberries play guitar? A jam session.

What do you get when you cross an apple with a shellfish? A crab apple.

What do you call a small, round green vegetable that breaks out of prison? An escape pea.

Why did the tomato blush? It saw the salad dressing.

Why do hamburgers go to the gym? To get better buns.

What do you get from a pampered cow? Spoiled milk.

Why did the cucumber need a lawyer? Because it was in a pickle.

What do you call a sheep covered in chocolate? A Hershey baa-aa-aah.

How do you burn 2000 calories in 20 minutes? Forget to

take the brownies out of the oven.

What is green and brown and crawls through the grass? A Girl Scout who lost her cookies.

What kind of candy do you eat on the school playground? Recess pieces.

How do you make a milkshake? Give it a good scare.

Did you hear about the big brawl at the Red Lobster? Battered shrimp were everywhere.

What is small, red, and whispers? A hoarse radish.

Where do cabbage and lettuce go to find a job? A headhunter.

What did the doctor tell the eggplant after his friend, the asparagus, was hit by a car? "He'll be a vegetable for the rest of his life."

How do you fix a broken pizza? With tomato paste.

What's the difference between a liberal arts graduate and a large pepperoni pizza? The large pizza can feed a family of four.

Why was the meat packer arrested? For bringing home the bacon.

Why did the Pepsi employee get fired? He tested positive for Coke.

That awkward moment when you spend $3 for a bottle of Evian and realize that spelled backward, it's naive.

Why did the Oreo go to the dentist? Because it lost its filling.

Why did the ice cream truck break down? Because of the Rocky Road.

Do you know what happens if you eat too much alphabet soup? You have a massive vowel movement.

5.

FOR THE KIDS

What do you call it when cowboys put on their clothes?
Ranch dressing.

Why doesn't the moon need a haircut? Because it waxes.

How does a volleyball team welcome their new
neighbors? With a block party.

Did you hear about the unstamped letter? You wouldn't
get it.

What happened to the frog who parked illegally? He got
toad.

What can you serve but never eat? A tennis ball.

What do you call a knight who is afraid to fight? Sir
Render.

Did you hear about the kids who wanted to visit

Washington, DC this summer? Their Dad thought that was a capital idea.

What did the mermaid use to clean her tail? Tide.

What do you call an alligator in a vest? An investigator.

What rock group has four guys who don't sing? Mount Rushmore.

What do you sing at a snowman's birthday party? Freeze A Jolly Good Fellow.

Why did the clock get kicked out of the library? It tocked too much.

What kind of fish bait do librarians use? Bookworms.

What happened to the glue the man ordered online? It got stuck in the mail.

What's Jack Frost's favorite school subject? Alegebrrrrrr...

What's a pirate's favorite school subject? Arrrrrrrrrrt...

Where do you park on the Moon? Anywhere you can find space, or at the parking meteor.

Where does a dad keep all his jokes? In a dadabase.

What do you call the superhero with a bad sense of direction? Wander Woman.

Did you hear about the bald guy who still carries a comb? He just can't part with it.

What do you get when you dump a bunch of books into the ocean? A title wave.

Do you want a brief explanation of what an acorn is? In a nutshell, it's an oak.

What did the beach say when the tide came in? Long time, no sea.

Did you hear that the Terminator retired? He's now the exterminator.

What did the inventor of the walkie-talkie call a nightmare? A screamie-dreamie.

What do you call a man who can't stand? Neil.

What do you call a flower that runs on electricity? A power plant.

What do you call a sword that doesn't weigh very much? A light saber.

Did you hear about the dyslexic zombie? He eats only Brians.

What does a vegetarian zombie eat? Graaaaains!

What do you call a girl standing in the middle of a volleyball court? Annette.

What do you call a fake noodle? An impasta.

I don't trust the stairs. They're always up to something.

Why did the coffee file a police report? It got mugged.

How do trees access the internet? They log in.

What do you call a dog who does magic tricks? A Labracadabrador.

Why did the pig have to stop exercising? He pulled a hammy.

Did you hear about the man who was afraid of elevators? He's taking steps to avoid them.

Why couldn't the bicycle stand up by itself? It was two tired.

How does NASA organize a party? They planet.

What do you call a cow with no legs? Ground beef.

What do you call a two-legged cow? Lean beef.

Did you hear about the woman who had all her lamps stolen? She was delighted.

I was listening to a song about superglue yesterday. It's been stuck in my head ever since.

If a child refuses to take a nap, is she guilty of resisting arrest?

Why did the scarecrow receive an award? Because he was outstanding in his field.

Why did the cowboy buy a dachshund? Someone told him to get a long little doggie.

What did the clock do when it was hungry? It went back four seconds.

What did the buffalo say when his calf left for school? Bi-son.

What's it called when you have too many aliens? Extra-terrestrials.

What do you call cheese that isn't yours? Nacho cheese.

Why was the math book so sad? Because it had so many problems.

How does Darth Vader like his toast? On the dark side.

What's the best time to go to the dentist. Tooth hurty.

What kind of music do astronauts like? Neptunes.

Where did the pirate get his hook? From the second-hand store.

What's the difference between a hippo and a zippo? One is extremely big and heavy, and the other is a little lighter.

Why did the football coach go to the bank? To get his

quarter back.

How do celebrities stay so cool? They have lots of fans.

What did the fisherman say to the magician? Pick a cod, any cod.

Why don't eggs tell jokes? Because they'd crack each other up.

What do you call a dinosaur that crashes his car? Tyrannosaurus Wrecks.

Did you hear about the pregnant bed bug? She's having her baby in the spring.

Which hand is better to write with? Neither. It's better to use a pencil.

Why did Humpty-Dumpty have a great fall? To make up for his miserable summer.

What washes up on really small beaches? Micro-waves.

How do you talk to giants? Use big words.

How do you stop an astronaut's baby from crying? You rocket.

Which superhero hits the most home runs? Batman.

Why was the painting sent to jail? It was framed.

Why can't you trust atoms? They make up everything.

Did you hear about the restaurant on the moon? Great food, no atmosphere.

Why can't you hear a pterodactyl go to the bathroom? Because the pee is silent.

What do you call a pony with a sore throat? A little horse.

What do you get when you cross a turtle with a porcupine? A slowpoke.

What do you call a pig who knows karate? A pork chop.

What has four wheels and flies? A garbage truck.

What's the smartest insect? The spelling bee.

Why do bees have sticky hair? They use a honeycomb.

What goes tick-tock woof-woof? A watchdog.

Why do shoemakers go to heaven? They have good soles.

Why won't dinosaurs eat clowns? They taste funny.

Why did the first-grader bring a ladder to school? He wanted to go to high school.

Why was the broom late? It overswept.

How do you identify a dogwood tree? By its bark.

What did the stamp say to the envelope? Stick with me and we'll go places.

What do you call a sleeping cow? A bulldozer.

Why can't Cinderella play soccer? Because she is always running away from the ball.

What did one toilet say to the other? You look a bit flushed.

A ham sandwich walks into a bar and orders a beer. The bartender says, 'Sorry we don't serve food here.

6.

HALLOWEEN JOKES

What's a witch's favorite school subject? Spelling.

What do you get when you cross a stern teacher with a vampire? Lots of blood tests.

What sound does a witch's motorcycle make? Broom, broom.

Do you know why ghosts hate rainy Halloweens? Rain always dampens the spirits.

Why do ghosts make good cheerleaders? They have a lot of spirit.

What's a vampire's least favorite meal? Steak.

Why do werewolves join the Cub Scouts? For the Pack meetings.

What happened to the man who didn't pay his exorcist?

He was repossessed.

Satan was furious when he went bald. There was hell toupee.

What's a mummy's favorite music? Wrap.

Why does no one like Count Dracula? He's a real pain in the neck.

Why didn't the skeleton go to the Halloween party? He had no body to go with.

What did the skeleton bring to the potluck dinner? Spare ribs.

How do you mend a broken Jack-O-Lantern? With a pumpkin patch.

Why didn't the skeleton go to school? His heart wasn't in it.

What's the tallest structure in Transylvania? The Vampire State Building.

What do vampires drive? Blood mobiles.

How does a vampire start a letter? Tomb it may concern.

What's the best way to get rid of a demon? Exorcise.

Where does a ghost vacation? Mali-Boo.

Why do vampires us so much mouthwash? Bat breath.

What's a goblins favorite cheese? Monster-ella.

What kind of pants do ghosts wear? Boo Jeans.

Why did the game warden arrest the ghost? He didn't have a haunting license.

What do monsters grill at the cookout? Frankenfurters.

Why did the ghost go to the liquor store? To get some boos.

What is a skeleton's favorite French leader? Napoleon Bone Apart.

Why did Frankenstein go to a therapist? He thought he had a screw loose.

What's a vampire's favorite dog? A bloodhound.

What do cows hate to get in their Halloween bags? Milk Duds.

What Halloween candy is a zombie's favorite? Lifesavers.

Two ghosts walk into a bar and the bartender says, "sorry, we don't serve spirits."

What do you call a ghost's mom and dad? Transparents.

What do you call a haunted chicken? A poultrygeist.

What happened when the werewolf swallowed a clock?

He got ticks.

What's a ghost's favorite party game? Hide and go shriek.

Why don't mummies go on vacation? They are afraid they'll relax and unwind.

What did his friends say when the zombie's fingers fell off while trick or treating? Butterfingers.

What kind of roads does a ghost haunt? Dead ends.

What did the witch do when she broke her broom? She had to witch-hike.

What do you call a cheesy Halloween dance? The Muenster Mash.

Where does a ghost swim? The Dead Sea.

What do goblins drink? Ghoul-Aid.

What position does a monster play in hockey? Ghoulie.

What do you call a dancing ghost? Polka-Haunt-Us.

What's a vampire's favorite fast food? A guy with high blood pressure.

Why did the witch stay overnight at the swanky hotel? She wanted Broom Service.

What do skeletons say before dinner? Bone Appetit!

What did one vampire say to another as they passed the morgue? Let's stop in for a cold one.

What do you get if you cross a dinosaur with a witch? Tyrannosaurus Hex.

Why was the wizard rushed to the hospital? He had a staff infection.

What's a vampire's favorite fruit? Neck-tarines.

What's a monster's favorite treat? Ghoul Scout cookies.

What kind of art do skeletons like? Skullptures.

What tattoo did the motorcycle-riding skeleton get? Bone to be wild.

What's a vampire's favorite holiday? Fangsgiving.

What do you call two witches who share an apartment? Broommates.

How is a bad boss like Satan? He's always ready to fire you.

What do demons have for breakfast? Devilled eggs.

What did the werewolf's mom say to him before he left for school? Don't forget to brush your face!

What spell does a wizard use to fill up his gas tank? Expecto petroleum!

What's a monster's favorite dessert? I Scream!

What monster plays tricks on Halloween? Prankenstein.

Where do baby ghosts go during the daytime? Day Scare Centers.

7.

LOVE, MARRIAGE, AND DIVORCE JOKES

What is the penalty for bigamy? Two mothers-in-law.

Love: the quest; Marriage: the conquest; Divorce: the inquest.

I divorced my cross-eyed wife. She was seeing someone on the side.

What's the difference between a husband and childbirth? One can be terribly painful and sometimes almost unbearable while the other is just having a baby.

Marriage is like deleting all the apps on your phone except one.

Why did the woman keep studying her marriage license? She was looking for the expiration date.

Did you hear about the man whose fiancée poked him in the eye? He stopped seeing her for a while.

Some say marriage is like a deck of cards. In the beginning, all you need is two hearts and a diamond. By the end, you wish you had a club and a spade.

My doctor told me I needed to break a sweat every day. So, I've decided to start lying to my wife.

My ex-girlfriend and I lived in adjacent houseboats. But we drifted apart.

Why shouldn't you marry a pro tennis player? Because love means nothing to them.

Did you hear about the girl who lost her engagement ring on the golf course? It was a diamond in the rough.

My wife ran off with my best friend last week. I miss him.

What's the difference between love and divorce? Love is grand. Divorce is one hundred grand.

What's the difference between love and marriage? Love is blind and marriage is a real eye-opener.

Why did the Mormon cross the road? To get to the other bride.

What do you call two spiders who have just gotten married? Newly-webs.

Did you hear about the bed bugs who just got engaged? They're getting married in the spring.

What does it mean when a man opens the car door for his wife? Either the car or the wife is new.

All marriages are happy. It's living together afterward that causes all the trouble.

When a man of 60 marries a girl of 21, it's like buying a book for someone else to read.

Nobody is perfect...until you fall in love with them.

The difference between secretaries and wives is:

Secretaries get a little behind at work; wives get a big behind at home.

Did you hear about the dwarf married couple? They struggled all their lives to put food on the table.

Love is never angry. Love is always patient. How many times do I have to tell you that?

If you want to read about love and marriage, you've got to buy two separate books.

I was married for a short time...just long enough to realize that all those comedians weren't joking.

Marriage is a wonderful institution, but who wants to live in an institution

I have a devoted wife who lets me give it to her both ways...Cash or Credit.

All men make mistakes, but married men find out about them sooner.

See no evil, hear no evil, date no evil.

With the divorce, I got custody of the kids and she got custody of the money.

If you have a headache, take an aspirin, if you have a pain in the ass, break up with them.

What's all the fuss about same-sex marriages? I've been

married for years, and I keep having the same sex.

The nicest thing about a nudist wedding is you don't have to ask – you can see who the best man is.

My wife and I finally became sexually compatible...we now achieve simultaneous headaches.

My husband and I divorced over religious differences – He thought he was God.

The only reason my wife has an orgasm is so she'll have something else to moan about.

I haven't spoken to my wife in 18 months. She gets mad if I interrupt her.

I'm dating a homeless woman. It's easier to talk her into staying over.

My girlfriend always laughs during sex — no matter what she's reading.

Nothing in the world is more expensive than a woman who's free for the weekend.

What do you call it when your wife is wearing her sexiest lingerie? Laundry day.

Marriages are made in heaven. But, again, so are thunder, lightning, tornados, and hail.

Before marriage, a man yearns for the woman he loves.

After marriage, the 'Y' becomes silent.

Why do men like to fall in love at first sight? Because doing so saves them a lot of money.

Never laugh at your wife's choices. You are one of them.

8.

MUSIC JOKES

Why did Beethoven get rid of his chickens? All they said was, "Bach, Bach, Bach ..."

What happened to Beethoven after he died? He began decomposing.

A sign at a music shop: "Gone Chopin. Bach in a minuet."

What's Beethoven's favorite fruit? Ba-Na-Na-Na!

What did the drummer name his twin daughters? Anna One and Anna Two.

What's the difference between a savings bond and a musician? Eventually, a savings bond will mature and earn some money.

How do you fix a broken tuba? Use a tuba glue.

What message was on Bach's answering machine?

"Phone broken. Call Bach later."

Why are pirates such good singers? They can hit the high Cs.

What's the difference between accordion players and terrorists? Terrorists have sympathizers.

How do you make a bandstand? Take the chairs away.

What tone does a piano falling down a mineshaft make? A flat minor.

What do you call a beautiful woman on a tuba player's arm? A tattoo.

Why couldn't the string quartet find their favorite composer? He was Haydn.

What happens when you play country music backward? You get your truck, your dog, and your girlfriend back, and you stop drinking.

Did you hear about U2's lawyer? He works pro Bono.

Jazz isn't dead. It just smells funny.

A gentleman is someone who knows how to play the bagpipes but doesn't.

What do you call a musician without a girlfriend? Homeless.

You have Van Gogh's ear for music.

What will you never hear someone say about a banjo player? There's his Rolls Royce.

I've stopped listening to Wagner. I kept getting the urge to conquer Poland.

What kind of a band doesn't play music? A rubber band.

How do you make a musician's car more aerodynamic? Remove the Domino's sign.

If it ain't baroque, don't fix it.

What makes music in your hair? A headband.

Why is an icy sidewalk like music? If you don't C Sharp, you'll B Flat.

What's the difference between an accordion and an onion? No one cries when you chop an accordion into little pieces.

What do a viola and lawsuit have in common? Everyone's relieved when the case is closed.

What kind of music do balloons fear? Pop music.

Did you hear about the musician whose car was keyed? The damage appears to B minor.

What was the name of the original boy band? The Bach Street Boys.

Why shouldn't you let your children watch Big Band

performances on TV? Too much sax and violins.

Did you hear about the new cover band? It's called Duvet.

Why did the thieves rob the music store? For the lute.

What's a golfer's favorite type of music? Swing.

Why didn't Handel go shopping? Because he was Baroque.

What's the definition of perfect pitch? It's when you throw an accordion into a dumpster and hit a banjo.

There are so many jokes about famous classical composers that I could write you a Liszt.

What do they call Miley Cyrus in Europe? Kilometry Cyrus.

Why did the failed opera singer become a pirate? So she could finally hit the high Cs.

9.

OH, THAT'S SO DAD

Did you hear about the man who swallowed a handful of Scrabble tiles? His next trip to the bathroom spelled disaster.

Why did the girl hit her birthday cake with a sledgehammer? It was a pound cake.

What gym has instructors go door-to-door telling people about the benefits of joining? Jehovah's Fitness.

One of the Russian acrobats in our human pyramid has been deported. We don't have Oleg to stand on.

What type of magazines do cows read? Cattlelogs.

Why did the Uber driver cancel his gym membership? Because he didn't even Lyft, bro.

What do you call the droid that always takes a long way home? R2 Detour.

How do you get a country girl's attention? A tractor.

Did you hear about the man who tried drag racing? He says it's murder running in heels.

What did the pirate say on his 80th birthday? AYE MATEY!

What do bald sea captains worry most about? Cap sizes.

What do you get when you put a duck in the cement mixer? Quacks in the pavement.

Did you hear about the woman drinking a milkshake on a cliff? It was ledge 'n dairy.

What happened to the butcher when he backed into the meat grinder? He got a little behind in his work.

Air at the gas station used to be free, now it's $1.50. Must be inflation.

While walking home, I passed a lemon bar, a doughnut, and some Key Lime pie. That street was strangely desserted.

Your school years fly by. In 2020, they are going to ZOOM.

Why was the blonde staring at the orange juice box? Because it said, "concentrate."

Did you hear about the Italian chef who joined the Army? He wanted a pizza the action.

Why does the ocean roar? You would too if you had crabs on your bottom.

What do you call a fairy who doesn't shower? Stinker Bell.

Why did the woman wear a helmet to the dinner table? She was on a crash diet.

What did the banana say to the judge? I plan to win this case on a peel.

I just saw a guy shot by a paintball gun. He dyed on impact.

What do you drink if you want to get your rear in shape? Acetone.

What is a Russian wedding called? A Soviet union.

Want to hear a ceiling joke? It's over your head.

I was attacked by a gang with obsessive-compulsive disorder. Talk about organized crime.

What does a condiment wizard perform? Saucery.

Two peanuts were walking down the street. One was a salted.

What did the horse say after it tripped? "Help! I've fallen and I can't giddyup!"

Why didn't the quarter roll down the hill with the nickel? It had more cents.

What do you call a lonely cheese? Provolone.

Why is becoming a pirate so addictive? Once you lose your first hand, you're hooked.

What do you call an old man with great hearing? Deaf defying.

How do you tell the difference between a frog and a horny toad? A frog says, "Ribbit, ribbit" and a horny toad says, "Rub it, rub it."

What is the hair stylist's favorite exercise? Curls.

Why did the golfer change his pants? Because he got a hole in one.

What's blue and doesn't weigh much? Light blue.

What kind of shoes do Ninjas wear? Sneakers.

Why did the seafood chef quit going to the gym? He pulled a mussel.

What do you call a fat psychic? A four-chin teller.

What do you call it when several apes start a company? Monkey business.

Why do nurses like red crayons? Because they often have to draw blood.

What has ears but can't hear? A cornfield.

Why do candles always go on top of the cake? It's too hard to light them from the bottom.

What do you call an ugly dinosaur? An eyesaur.

In what order did the 26 letters go swimming? Alphawetical.

What do you call guys who love math? Algebros.

Why don't pirates shower before walking the plank?
Because they'll just wash up on shore later.

What sound do porcupines make when they kiss? Ouch!

Dogs can't operate MRI machines, but catscan.

What's a crafty dancer's favorite hobby? Cutting a rug.

What kind of a car does a sheep drive? A Lamborghini.

Did you hear about the two pieces of bread that got
married? It was loaf at first sight.

What kind of math do trees love? Twigonometry.

For years, my parents sent me to see a child
psychologist. That kid was no help at all.

What do you call an indecisive insect? A may-bee.

Why do dads tell such bad jokes? They want to help
their kids become groan ups.

What do you call two octopi that look the same?
Itentacle.

What has one head, one foot, and four legs? A bed.

What do you call an unpredictable camera? A loose
Canon.

Where do you go to learn to make banana splits? Sundae
school.

What's at the bottom of the ocean and shivers? A nervous wreck.

Did you hear about the man who had a horrible nightmare about earthquakes? He woke up trembling.

What do sprinters eat before a race? Nothing. They fast.

Did you hear about the new dating service in Prague? It's called Czech-Mate.

What did one Doritos farmer say to the other? Cool Ranch!

What does a cloud wear beneath his raincoat? Thunderwear.

How does a cucumber become a pickle? It goes through a jarring experience.

How does a scientist freshen her breath? With experi-mints.

What's worse than finding a worm in your apple? Finding half a worm.

I went to the plastic surgery addicts group meeting tonight. There were a lot of new faces there.

What's red and bad for your teeth? A brick.

What's a tornado's favorite game? Twister.

Did you hear about the priest with a secret life? He has an altar ego.

What did the Dalmatian say after lunch? That hit the spot.

Did you hear that Aristotle, Plato, and Socrates have formed a new band? It's called Rock of Sages.

What goes down but doesn't come back up? A yo.

What's the difference between a tennis ball and the Prince of Wales? One's heir to the throne, the other is thrown into the air.

Why was the Autopsy Club so excited? It was Open Mike Night.

What do you call a person in a tree with a briefcase? A branch manager.

Why did the kid cross the playground? To get to the other slide.

Did you hear about the bacon cheeseburger that couldn't stop telling jokes? It was on a roll.

What do prisoners use to call each other? Cell phones.

Why did the hamburger start working out? He wanted bigger buns.

What's Ironman without the suit? Stark naked.

Did you hear about the single guy with no kids who tells dad jokes? He's a faux pa.

What do you call someone who is really into stationary bikes? A cyclepath.

I heard someone at the gym trying to convince another guy that yoga is good exercise. Personally, I think it's kind of a stretch.

My wife is furious at our next-door neighbor who sunbathes topless in her backyard. Personally, I'm on the fence.

Did you hear about the man who works out religiously? Once at Easter and once at Christmas.

What happens if the average number of bullies at a school goes up? The mean increases.

Why did Charles Darwin begin working out? Because he believed in survival of the fittest.

Did you hear that the man who invented autocorrect died? May he restaurant in piece.

Why did the depressed man start bench pressing? He had some things he needed to get off his chest.

My wife asked me to clear the table? I had to get a running start, but I made it.

What do they say about someone who is 10% Polish? He's a tad Pole.

What do you call it when you die and come back as a hillbilly? Reintarnation.

Did you hear about the man who took his pillow to the ER after dropping it? It has a concushion.

Someone complimented my parking today. Found a piece of paper under my windshield wiper that said "parking fine."

What do Mexican tenth graders read in their American literature class? Tequila Mockingbird.

I just replaced our bed with a trampoline. My wife is going to hit the ceiling.

What cereal puts in the most time at the gym? Shredded Wheat.

An apple pie costs $2.50 in Jamaica, $2.75 in the Caymans, and $2.95 in St. Kitts. These are the pie rates of the Caribbean.

What did the Buddhist monk say to the hot dog vendor?

Make me one with everything.

I think my wife is putting glue on my antique weapons? She denies it, but I'm sticking to my guns.

What did the librarian say when the books were in a mess? "We ought to be ashamed of our shelves."

Why did Satan go to the gym? To work on his 666 pack.

Did you know they have a special ceremony for bodybuilding priests? A muscle mass.

What do you call a hen that counts her own eggs? A mathemachicken.

How do you make holy water? You boil the hell out of it.

I'm reading a book about anti-gravity. It's impossible to put down!

I ordered a chicken and an egg from Amazon. I'll let you know.

Did you hear about the fat man who decided to identify as skinny? He's trans-slender.

It's Spring! I'm so excited, I've wet my plants.

What do you call a cannibal who keeps taking small bites out of his siblings? A munchkin.

I've recently taken up fencing. The neighbors say they are calling the police if I don't put it back.

What do you call an ant that has been shunned? A socially dissed ant.

Why were the people running towards Finland? It was a race to the Finnish.

Did you hear that Amazon has started a new service to deliver custom shirts within 48 hours? It's called Tailor Swift.

Two goats were munching on a movie script. The first goat said, "this is good." The second said, "the book was better."

Did you hear about the Vicks Vapo-Rub truck that overturned on I-95? Hard to believe, but there's no congestion for eight hours.

Have you met my friend from Prague who is a chess player? He's my Czech mate.

Did you hear about the skinny personal trainer who couldn't cut it? He had to put in his too weak notice.

How did Pharaoh enslave the Jews? He created a pyramid scheme.

What do you call a fortune teller who only sees the worst in things? A pessimystic.

Where do you stand at a party to hear jokes? The punch line.

What happens when you drink a bottle of bug repellent? Your fly stops working.

Did you hear about the man who discovered petroleum in his backyard? He is taking an oily retirement.

What machine should a 65-year-old man use to impress much younger women? An ATM.

Why don't cows ever skip leg day at the gym? Because they care about their calves.

Did you see the great documentary about perfume? It was on Chanel No. 5.

What should you do when you feel blue? Start breathing again.

What do you call a dictionary on drugs? High definition.

A Roman walked into a bar, held up two fingers, and said "5 beers please."

What do you call Hispanic men over 65 years of age? Señor citizens.

What comes out of a vending machine set up in a bathroom? John Candy.

What do you call a weight-loss mantra? Fat chants.

Why is tennis such a loud game? Because each player raises a racket.

What do you call a fat Chinese mystic? A four-chin teller.

Why did the woman fire her personal trainer? She was tired of all the ab use.

Did you hear about the girl who went to beauty college and flunked cosmetics? They let her take a make-up exam.

Why should you always guard your rear while you're in the hospital? You're in enema territory.

What's the difference between a hungry pirate and a drunken pirate? One has a rumbling tummy, and the other's a tumbling rummy.

Why wouldn't the man let his kids go to the new pirate movie? Because it was rated ARRRRRRRRR!

My uncle had a rabbit's foot for thirty years. His other foot was quite normal.

Dad, are we pyromaniacs? Yes, we arson.

Why did Stalin only write in lower case? He was afraid of Capitalism.

Bullets are weird. They only do their job after being fired.

Why can't dyslexics tell jokes? They always punch up the screw line.

What weighs more water or butane? Water, because

butane is lighter fluid.

Where is the first Bible mention of tennis? When Joseph served in Pharaoh's court.

Did you hear about the woman who went to the paint store to get thinner? It didn't work.

Why don't mathematicians consume alcohol? Because they can't drink and derive.

What's the difference between a well-dressed man on a unicycle and a poorly dressed man on a bicycle? Attire.

My New Year's resolution is to read more. So, I've turned on the TV's closed captioning.

What do you call a flirtatious philosopher? Socratease.

Did you hear about the 99-year-old who still doesn't need glasses? He drinks straight from the bottle.

What do you get when you cross the Atlantic with the Titanic? Halfway.

What do you call a disease you get from your Chinese martial arts instructor? Kung Flu.

What did the bra say to the hat? You go on a head, and I'll hang around with these boobs.

I have this terrible condition where I'm only happy at airports. My doctor says it is terminal.

What do you do with dead chemists? Barium.

What does the sign say at the vegan seafood buffet? Kelp yourself.

What's the greatest danger from a fire at a clock factory? Second-hand smoke.

I went to a smoke shop to discover that it had been replaced by an apparel store. Clothes but no cigar.

I told my suitcases there will be no vacation this year. Now I'm dealing with emotional baggage.

What do you call an apology written in dots and dashes? Re-Morse Code.

Who invented fractions? Henry the 1/8th.

Why did security stop the man with flame sleeve tattoos from entering the building? No fire arms allowed.

What did the feldspar boulder say to the quarry worker? Don't take me for granite.

Why was the fraction nervous about marrying the decimal? Because he would have to convert.

What did the bread dough say to the psychiatrist? My kneads aren't being met.

Why did the customer return the book on medical procedures? Because someone had removed the

Appendix.

What do you call laying on the beach covering up with your male children? Applying son screen.

Why did the zombie skip school? He was feeling rotten.

I bought some shoes from a drug dealer. Don't know what they're laced with but I've been tripping all day.

Why did the tomato go out with a prune? He couldn't find a date.

Did you hear about the new coffee shop comedy club? It's called Brew-Ha-Ha.

What do you call someone who tells dad jokes incessantly? A groan man.

What do you call a driver who has never had an accident? Wreckless.

What happens if you eat yeast and shoe polish? You'll rise and shine.

Do you know how to keep the dream alive? Keep hitting the snooze alarm.

I don't always roll a joint, but when I do it's usually my ankle.

Did you hear about the stoner who did a flip every time he took a puff off his joint? Turns out he was smoking tumbleweed.

Did you hear about the manic Irishman who always bounced off the walls? His name is Rick O'Shea.

How do you make a waterbed bouncier? Add spring water.

Did you know that Genghis Khan had a son who was electrocuted? Yep, Shocka Khan.

If dads get dad bods, what do priests get? Father figures.

Why does no one in Antarctica ever get sick? Because they're so ice-o-lated.

Who is India's favorite basketball player? Steph Curry.

What is Albert Einstein's rapper name? MC Squared.

How did the Irish jig get started? Too much Guinness and not enough bathrooms.

Why did it take Russia so long to recover after World War II? They kept Stalin around.

Did you hear about the magician who used sleight of hand to steal candy? He had more than a few Twix up his sleeve.

What did the homeless man's dog say? Man, this is the longest walk home ever.

What's the difference between "coma" and "comma"?

The length of the pause.

Why did the blonde get excited after finishing her puzzle in six months? The box said 2 – 4 years.

How does a dyslexic poet write? Inverse.

What type of people never get angry? Nomads.

Why do mermaids wear seashells? Because D-shells are too big.

What do you call a snail who falls off the turtle he is riding? Ex-cargo.

A mime broke his left arm in a bar fight. He still has the right to remain silent.

Did you know that Bruce Lee had a vegan brother? Broco Lee.

What do you call a Frenchman wearing beach sandals? Phillipe Phloppe.

What shoes do welfare recipients wear? Loafers.

10.

ON THE JOB JOKES

What happened when most dads started working from home? It started a pundemic.

How do we know that chefs are mean? They all beat eggs, slice up vegetables, and whip cream.

What kind of shoes do plumbers wear? Clogs.

Why did the counterfeiter quit his job? He wasn't making any real money.

Where are average things manufactured? In the satisfactory.

Why did the baker quit making doughnuts? He was tired of the hole thing.

How do priests stay fit? They exorcise.

My boss told me to have a good day. So, I went home.

How do you impress the baker's daughter? Bring her flours.

What does the dentist of the year get? A little plaque.

I've just started dating a girl who works at the zoo. I think she's a keeper.

Why did the invisible man turn down the job offer? He couldn't see himself doing it.

Did you hear about the man who started a business as a watchmaker? He wanted to set his own hours.

What do you call the coolest, hippest shoe repairman? Sole Man.

Who is the coolest person in the hospital? The hip doctor.

Why did the man break up with his baker girlfriend? She was too kneady.

How did Roman barbers cut hair? With a pair of Caesars.

Why should a man marry a young archaeologist? Because the older you get, the more interest she has in you.

I told my boss that I was having 'Deja-Moo'. That's the feeling that you've heard this bull before.

Why did the tree go to the dentist? For a root canal.

What is a chiropractor's favorite music? Hip pop.

Accomplishing the impossible means only that the boss will add it to your regular duties.

I don't want to achieve immortality through my work, I want to achieve immortality through not dying.

Ideas are great provided they don't degenerate into work.

Got a new job at the guillotine factory. I'll beheading there shortly.

I asked the barista why she was wearing a surgical mask. She said it was actually a coughy filter.

What did the scarecrow say about his job? It's not for everyone, but hay – it's in my jeans.

What do you call someone who makes bicycle wheels? A spokesperson.

I used to work at a fire hydrant factory. You couldn't find a parking place anywhere nearby.

Did you hear about the bakery that burned down? Now, that business is toast.

Why did the woman slap the electrician? He wanted to check her shorts.

Did you hear about the cross-eyed teacher who got fired? She couldn't control her pupils.

Did you hear about the banker who got fired? An old woman asked him to check her balance, so he pushed her over.

Did you hear about the taxi driver who got fired? Apparently, people didn't appreciate him going the extra mile.

What do dentists call X-rays? Tooth pics.

What did the doctor tell the patient who wanted to sew his own stitches? Suture self.

What did one elf say to the other when they walked into the dwarves' restaurant? Wow, they're really short-staffed.

A woman in labor suddenly shouted, "shouldn't, wouldn't, couldn't, didn't, can't." "Don't' worry," said the doctor. "Those are just contractions."

Did you hear about the farmer who made gloves from herbs? He had too much thyme on his hands.

Did you hear about the man who fell into the upholstery machine? He's fully recovered now.

Did you know Benedict Arnold worked on Wall Street? Yep, he was a day traitor.

Where does seaweed look for a job? In the newspaper's kelp wanted section.

Why did the guy who worked evenings moving suits of armor at the museum quit his job? He was tired of knight shifts.

The anesthetist offered to knock me out with gas or a boat paddle. It was an ether/oar proposition.

A patient told the doctor that he felt like a deck of cards. The doctor told him, "I'll deal with you later."

Did you hear about the guy who quit his job making origami? He was tired of all the paperwork.

A nap is healthy, and it really shortens the workday.

Middle age is when work is a lot less fun—and fun is a lot more work.

The bully still takes my lunch money. On the plus side, now he makes great Subway sandwiches.

Even a mosquito doesn't get a slap on the back until he starts to work.

All I want is less to do, more time to do it, and higher pay for not getting it done.

How come you've never seen a plumber bite his nails?

If those space scientists are so smart, why do they all count backward?

Most people work just enough not to get fired and get paid just enough not to quit.

11.

ONE-LINERS

Military barbers shave their privates.

Pollen is what happens when flowers can't keep it in their plants.

I started out with nothing, and I still have most of it.

I like long walks, especially when they're taken by people who annoy me.

If you hang yourself, you die of your own free will and a cord.

I don't know if I want to change the world or just toilet train it.

Well, here I am! What are your other two wishes?

If you think eggplant is good, you should try any other food; it's much better.

When life gives you melons you must be dyslexic.

It takes a lot of balls to golf the way I do.

My mother has schizophrenia, but she's good people.

The problem with kleptomaniacs is that they always take things literally.

Geology rocks, but geography's where it's at.

The best time to add insult to injury is when you're signing someone's cast.

My first experience with culture shock was when I peed on an electric fence.

A termite walks into the bar and asks, 'Is the bar tender here?'

The last thing I want to do is hurt you, but it's still on the list.

A recent study has found that women who carry a little extra weight live longer than the men who mention it.

When the cannibal showed up late to the buffet, they gave him the cold shoulder.

I'm on the whiskey diet and have already lost three days.

Anyone who told you to be yourself couldn't have given you worse advice.

Confidence is the feeling a person has before he fully understands the situation.

The first time I got a universal remote control, I thought to myself, 'This changes everything.'

The future, the present, and the past walk into a bar. Things got a little tense.

A ghost walked into a bar and ordered a shot of vodka. The bartender said, 'Sorry, we don't serve spirits here.'

Honesty is the best policy, but insanity is a better

defense.

Regular naps prevent old age...especially if you take them while driving.

I didn't think orthopedic shoes would help, but I stand corrected.

People who take care of chickens are literally chicken tenders.

6:30 is the best time on a clock, hands down.

Adam & Eve were the first ones to ignore the Apple terms and conditions.

Despite the high cost of living, it remains popular.

Well, to be Frank with you, I'd have to change my name.

Communist jokes aren't funny unless everyone gets them.

Two blondes walked into a bar...you'd think one of them would have seen it.

Even on the most exalted throne, you are still sitting on nothing but your ass.

The higher up the ladder you climb, the more your butt shows.

Shouldn't a self-addressed envelope be addressed to "Envelope"?

Never get into fights with ugly people, they have nothing to lose.

If electricity comes from electrons, does morality come from morons?

If at first you don't succeed, find out if the loser gets anything.

The Law of Common Sense – Never accept a drink from a urologist.

If love is blind, why is lingerie so popular?

If there's one thing I can't stand, it's intolerance.

Being overweight just sort of snacks up on you

Sign at a nudist colony: "Sorry, clothed for winter"

12.

TECHNOLOGY JOKES

Why did the PowerPoint presentation cross the road? To get to the other slide.

Did you know Apple is getting into vision care? They've introduced the iPatch.

How are a computer and a human different? A computer never blames another computer for its mistakes.

For a list of all the ways technology has failed to improve the quality of life, please press 3.

If it's really a supercomputer, how come the bullets don't bounce off when I shoot at it?

A television may insult your intelligence, but nothing rubs it in like a computer

What's a bad wizard's favorite computer program? Spell-check.

What do the kids say from the backseat of a time machine? Are we then yet?

Why did the computer go to the dentist? It had Bluetooth.

Why did the computer go to the doctor? It had a virus.

Why did the farmer move his modem to the barn? He wanted a stable wi-fi connection.

Why are iPhone chargers not called apple juice?

How does a computer get drunk? It takes screenshots.

Why was the computer late for work? It had a hard drive.

Autocorrect has become my worst enema.

What do you call a ride-sharing app that serves breakfast? Eggs Uber Easy.

How many programmers does it take to change a light bulb? None. It's a hardware problem.

Why did the computer crash? It had a bad driver.

Why did the waiter's computer not work? Server error.

Do you know the difference between a redneck and a computer? Rednecks have no trouble shooting.

What do you call having your grandmother on speed-dial? Instagram.

How are computers like air conditioning? They both stop operating correctly when you open windows.

Why did the man's Wi-Fi stop working? His neighbors forgot to pay the bill.

Girls are like Internet domain names. The ones I like are already taken.

What did the computer do at lunchtime? Had a byte.

Why did the Army officer smash his laptop? He heard

there was Intel inside.

What do you call security officers at a Samsung store? Guardians of the Galaxy.

Did you hear about the angry computer? He had a chip on his shoulder.

I accidentally called Alexa Siri and now neither talks to me.

Why can't computers play tennis? They are too busy surfing the net.

What do you get when you cross a dog and a computer? A machine with a bark worse than its byte.

What's the fastest cell phone provider? Sprint.

What do cell phones order at a bar? Apps.

I deleted all my German friends from my cell phone contact list. Now I'm Hans free.

My wife and I got married under a cell phone tower? The ceremony wasn't much but the reception was great.

I got a new cell phone for my wife. Pretty good trade if I do say so myself.

Why did the smartphone need glasses? Because it lost all its contacts.

I asked Siri why I was still single. She turned on the front camera.

13.

THE LAW

My lawyer told me to get my affairs in order? I asked, "Alphabetically or by age?"

Did you hear about the guy suspected of killing people by hitting them with a bag of cement? Police are looking for concrete evidence.

A Mafia hit-man has been arrested for killing a man in a rice field with a porcelain figurine. It's the first known case of a knick-knack paddywhack.

Why did the coffee call the police? It was mugged.

Did you hear about the two kids police arrested – one for drinking battery acid and the other for eating fireworks? They charged one and let the other off.

What do you call an attorney with an IQ of 75? Your honor.

Did you hear about the man bitten by a radioactive lawyer? Now he has power of attorney.

What do a recovering alcoholic and a law student have in common? They each must successfully pass the bar.

Did you hear about the man who survived mustard gas in battle and pepper spray from the police? He's now a seasoned veteran.

Why did police take the hospitalized patient into custody? He was under cardiac arrest.

At a marathon, police arrested someone for firing a starter's pistol. They believe it is race-related.

What did the lawyer say leaving the scene of the accident after being rear-ended? I'll be suing you.

Why didn't the cow take a job on the police force? He refused to go on steak outs.

What is a police officer's favorite color? Copper.

Did you hear about the attorney who opened a coffee shop inside his law office? It's called Grounds For Divorce.

Why couldn't the police catch the tree bandit? He had them stumped.

Did you hear about the farmer found dead in the chicken coop? Police suspect fowl play.

How many lawyers does it take to change a light bulb? Three. One to climb the ladder, one to push it over, and a third to sue the ladder company.

When the cop asked if he had a police record what did the man say? "No, but I have a couple of Sting albums."

Ninety-nine percent of all lawyers give the rest a bad name.

What do you call a priest who also is an attorney? Father-in-law.

How does a sheep become a lawyer? He must pass the ba-aa-aah.

What's the difference between an onion and a lawyer? You cry when you cut up the onion.

Did you hear about the man kidnapped by a gang of mimes? It was an unspeakable act.

What does a lawyer wear? A lawsuit.

Did you hear about the truck full of wigs that turned over on the Interstate? Police are still combing the area.

A cement mixer collided with a prison van. Be on the lookout for hardened criminals.

Did you hear about the album done by convicts? It's a criminal record.

Why did the burglar kick in his own door? To see if he liked working from home.

What's the difference between a female attorney and a pitbull? Lipstick.

Did you hear about the man who had been searching for three years for his mother-in-law's killer? Apparently, no one will do it.

Why was the lawyer on his deathbed reading the Bible? He was looking for loopholes.

Police have arrested the world tongue-twister champion. If found guilty he'll be given a tough sentence.

What did the lawyer say to convince the judge his penguin client should be released on bail? "Clearly, he is not a flight risk."

Did you hear about the skydiving photographer the police arrested? Charged him with in-descent exposure.

Did you hear about the man who attacked the toy shop owner? He was charged with assault. Battery was not included.

I stole a lawyer's underwear right before his court appearance. No way he'll succeed without his legal briefs.

What's a lawyer's favorite food? Anything battered.

Did you hear about the man stealing wheels off police cars? Cops are working tirelessly to catch him.

Did you hear about the giant fly terrorizing the westside? Police sent in a SWAT team.

What's the difference between lawyer and a leech? The leech stops sucking your blood after you're dead.

Did you hear that someone stole all the toilets at the police station? The cops have nothing to go on.

There are two kinds of lawyers. Those who know the

law and those who know the judge.

14.

VICES JOKES

Charles Dickens walks into a bar and says "I'll have a Martini." The bartender asks "Olive or Twist?"

Alcohol is a perfect solvent: It dissolves marriages, families, and careers.

An amnesiac walks into a bar. He goes up to a beautiful young woman and says, "So, do I come here often?"

Studies show that one in seven friends has a gambling addiction. My money is on Dave.

What's the difference between prayer in a casino and prayer in a church? In a casino, you really mean it.

You've been a bad girl. Go to my room.

I often feel like a 20-year-old. But there's never one around.

Two five-dollar bills walk into a bar and the bartender tells them that this is a singles bar.

Sex is the only activity where you start at the top and work your way to the bottom while getting a raise.

A conscience does not prevent sin. It only prevents you from enjoying it.

A doctor tells a woman she can no longer touch anything alcoholic. So she gets a divorce.

I was cheating on my wife with my blonde

secretary…She found lipstick on my collar, covered with White-Out.

What's the difference between men and pigs? Pigs don't turn into men when they drink.

I'd walk a mile for one of your smiles…and even farther for that thing you do with your tongue.

Life would be very empty if you had nothing to regret.

I'd really like to see how you look when I'm naked.

Last night, the sex was so good that even the neighbors had a cigarette.

To stop smoking is simple. I ought to know, I've done it a thousand times.

My boyfriend has no trouble committing . . . adultery.

It is now proved beyond doubt that smoking is one of the leading causes of statistics.

The only way to have safe sex is to abstain…from drinking.

I've never had a problem with drugs; I've had problems with the police.

I never worry about being driven to drink; I just worry about being driven home.

"Just say no!" prevents teenage pregnancy the way

"Have a nice day" cures chronic depression.

I drink so much, the last time I gave a urine sample, there was an olive in it.

I've been smoking for thirty years now and there's nothing wrong with my lung.

Let's have a party and invite your pants to come on down.

I think sex is better than logic, but I can't prove it.

A screwdriver goes into a bar. The bartender says, "Hey, we have a drink named after you!" The screwdriver asks, "You have a drink named Philip?"

I just read an article about the dangers of drinking that scared the crap out of me. That's it. No more reading!

A minister, a priest and a rabbi walk into a bar. "What is this," asks the bartender, "some kind of joke?"

I said "no" to drugs, but they just wouldn't listen.

When I drink alcohol everyone says I'm an alcoholic, but when I drink Fanta, no one says I'm fantastic.

A dog with his leg wrapped in bandages hobbles into a saloon. He sidles up to the bar and announces, "I'm lookin' fer the man that shot my paw."

ABOUT HARRY HOOVER

I am Harry Hoover, a self-improvement author, writer-for-hire, and speaker.

I've been a radio and newspaper journalist, covering cops and courts, a daily call-in talk show host, served as a columnist and managing editor, as well as a color commentator for UNCC basketball. Most recently, I owned an ad agency, which I sold to my business partner in 2015 so I could devote more time to writing.

Although my first book is called *Moving To Charlotte: The Un-Tourist Guide*, I consider it a self-improvement book, too. Our town offers great jobs, superb outdoor recreational opportunities, varied housing options, as well as interesting urban and suburban neighborhoods. A move here is a step toward self-improvement.

Born Creative: Free Your Mind, Free Yourself is my second book. This book helps you learn how to free your mind from societal influences so you can plan the life you desire. And, it's free.

Get Glad: Your Practical Guide To A Happier Life helps you understand why you aren't happy and provides highly actionable ideas on how to get happier a little at a time.

The *Dad's Book Of Jokes* could be considered a self-improvement book. There's nothing like laughter to improve your mood.

If you'd like more motivational and self-improvement tips, visit me here, https://medium.com/@harryhoover.

My wife, Terry, a mystery author, and I live near Lake Norman, North Carolina. We're blessed to be close to our son and grandsons.

Made in the USA
Middletown, DE
09 February 2022

60889323R00064